FROM
HOMELESSNESS
TO
RUBBING ELBOWS
WITH EXECUTIVES

Overcoming Adversity, Building New Skills, and
Living Out Your Dreams Based on Your Values

SCOTT A. NORCROSS

Author and Life Coach

authorHOUSE®

AuthorHouse™
1663 Liberty Drive
Bloomington, IN 47403
www.authorhouse.com
Phone: 1 (800) 839-8640

Published by AuthorHouse 12/16/2016

ISBN: 978-1-5246-5546-4 (sc)
ISBN: 978-1-5246-5545-7 (e)

Print information available on the last page.

This book is printed on acid-free paper.

Contact Information

Author	: *Scott Norcross*
Phone	: *612-267-4881*
Website	: *www.scottnorcross.com*

Contents

Preface

Have you ever wondered how you can overcome your challenges and live a more joyful and rewarding life? Maybe you're wondering how you can explore and define your own personal values. Would you like to explore how you can live a life based on your values? Would you like to take steps in achieving your dreams?

I would like to take you on a journey of my experiences in these areas, as we explore some insights that I have gained to these questions and more. Some insights and learnings are good. While others may not be categorized as good. However, they are also beneficial. Some insights and learnings even need to be undone, unlearned and reversed to achieve healthy thinking and be in alignment with our personal values.

Thank you for purchasing this book. You may ask, what qualifies me to write this book? A hard knock life and a very personal journey qualifies me. I was once homeless. This was one struggle of many. I desperately needed to find a new kind of life to live. I had little to no marketable skills, and found myself in a very desperate situation. It seemed like no one cared enough to help, family and friends alike. Nor was it their responsibility to help. It was a very lonely and scary place to be and my family and I felt stuck.

As a young man who was homeless, I spat in the face of adversity, challenges and struggles and worked diligently to survive and overcome. I have moved from homelessness to building new skills, improved myself throughout the years, paid my dues and ended up working side by side with executives in small companies, large corporations, and government organizations. Now I am living out my long term dreams.

I have now become an Author, and Life Coach. My desire is to encourage and inspire others to heal, improve, and live a life based on their values, while working toward living out their dreams. If I can do it, so can you!

With the purchase of this book, I am offering my readers a way to connect with me as well as connecting with other readers through a very low cost monthly membership. You can access the social media site that I have setup. Go to www.scottnorcross.com to sign-up. Customers with a membership, will get a 10% discount on all Life Coaching services.

If you would like to sign up for life coaching services, you can do that at www.scottnorcross.com. You will get a free 30-minute initial coaching session when you sign up. No long-term commitments necessary.

Chapter 1: What Are Your Personal Values

 To live your life based on your values, you must know, have explored and identified your own personal values. Remember, these values are yours. You are a unique individual so you don't need to base it on someone else or compare yourself with another person.

So what does this process take? It takes an approach to be totally honest with yourself about what your true personal values are. They are not what you wish they were, but what your values actually are.

I am going to give some examples about what some potential values are, however this is not an exhaustive list.

Accepting Yourself	Achieving	Admiring
Appreciation	Asking for Help	Being Compassionate
Being Truthful	Belonging	Connecting
Creating	Daring to Dream	Dancing with Joy
Embracing the Moment	Feeling Different	Feeling Pleasure
Feeling Secure	Feeling Peace	Forgiving
Imagining	Letting It Be	Loving and Being Loved
Moving	Saying Goodbye	Seeing Possibilities
Seeking Freedom	Seeking Knowledge	Seeking Wisdom
Staying with Uncertainty	Struggling	Trusting
Understanding		

Feel free to add your own values to the list of suggestions that fit within your own value system. Then order them by order of importance to you.

Chapter 2: Hard Times Ahead

My family and I lived on the east coast. My family that I grew up with had very colorful humor to say the least. We had moments of fun, and challenge mixed with very interesting dynamics. That is putting it nicely.

My parents had no formal education and never had the capacity to make a great salary, however, they certainly did the best that they could with what they had to work with. My mother, Renee' was a waitress and she was only able to work sporadically. Mom was kind, forgiving, compassionate and would give someone whatever she had if they were in need. My father Earle worked in restaurants, fast food, or factories. He was quite colorful to say the least.

Dad was humorous, liked to tease and goof around. He was also kind in many ways. However, just like anyone else, we all had our character flaws. Sometime, Earle would carry his teasing too far and hurt people's feelings.

> **Insight #1: Be careful how you play and tease. You could hurt people if you take things too far or are insensitive to other people.**

Growing up, I didn't get to see my grandparents often since my father didn't get along with his in-laws. This is certainly not uncommon.

You really have to deal with the cards your dealt in terms of those relationships and it does affect everyone.

When I did go over to my grandparent's house, I had a very good time. I felt warm, safe and loved. I felt like I could just be me, a kid. They would sit me down, and serve me milk and cookies. I still remember the wood stained, treat cabinet. They were a wealthy family compared to us.

Our family was quite poor and didn't even make it financially. Living from paycheck to paycheck would have been an improvement.

My parents never owned their own home, and never owned a car. I can't even remember a time that we went on any family vacations. We couldn't afford vacations and life did not really offer us those kinds of luxuries. There were bigger needs that had to be attended to. You don't miss what you don't have.

> Insight #2: Life is all work and business and not much about play. Little did I know later in life, that I would have to learn how to play.

Eventually, mom developed spinal arthritis and was unable to work most of the time, so we ended up consistently being a one income family which led to further financial disaster. We depended on my father's income alone. We did get by financially as a family for many years, sometimes with the help of food shelves and food stamps.

While all these things were happening, there were disagreements about money. My mother enjoyed Bingo which was her only outlet from all the problems and chaos we had.

> Insight #3: It is OK to hide and lie for the sake of the family and finances. I chose not to believe that.

> **Insight #4: There is no such thing as fighting fair and it always includes raising your voice and swearing. I have had to unlearn this.**

I remember the times when it was pouring rain outside, and my father would put his raincoat on and ride his bike in the pouring rain in order to get to work to support his family. In spite of all the challenges, difficulties, lack of knowledge and dysfunction, he loved his family and tried his best to support us.

> **Insight #5: Do all that you can, to love and support your family, regardless of the challenges and difficulties.**

I had two brothers, and they were older, grown up and on their own with their own families to support. At home, it was just my parents and I. Little did we know, we thought we had it rough but there were even tougher times ahead, filled with many more challenges and much adversity.

Early on in my life, I had no marketable skills and was only fourteen years-old. My only real enjoyment in life at this time was playing guitar, singing and watching professional wrestling.

Life was becoming tougher as our expenses grew, and my father's job changes were causing a decline in our family income. We felt like our world was crumbling in on us and we felt cursed. My brothers stated that there was a Norcross curse and I started believing that due to our difficult unpleasant life. I believed that we were very cursed people and life would always be this way.

We didn't even know how to think about our development, or personal values. It was never even something that was on our radar. Our dreams no longer mattered and didn't even seem like much of a possibility anymore, so why bother dreaming. We were afraid of what was to come next. We could see the writing on the wall and we were afraid of what was yet to come.

Insight #6: Dreams were not achievable. Just get by in life and survive. I had to unlearn this.

Chapter 3: More Adversity and Illness

Things were getting increasingly difficult and the only way that we could buy anything was on rent to own purchases. I still remember that the person from the rent to own store would come to the house to collect the weekly payment.

Some weeks my father did not have the money and he would turn off all the lights, turn off the television and he would tell us to be quiet. When he was sure the bill collector left, we could resume what normal living was for us. Other times, we would leave the house and go up the street for breakfast to avoid the bill collector. Sometimes that was the highlight of the week.

> **Insight #7: It is fine to be deceptive in managing finances and even be irresponsible if needed, as long as it benefits my wallet. I needed to unlearn this message.**

We were getting further behind with our rent. I overheard a conversation that my parents were having in the apartment with the landlord. The landlord was telling my parents that he has been doing what he can to keep our family in the apartment but if we didn't start making more progress to get caught up with the rent, that he would have no option but to evict us. He expressed not wanting to do that but he would evict us if it were necessary.

My parents were very worried, felt bad and knew that there was no way on God's Green Earth that we were going to catch up. There were many factors to our family's financial disaster.

Between my mother having spinal arthritis and not having the ability to work due to not being able to stand for extended periods of time and my father's earning potential, we were sinking fast. We were getting food stamps, getting help from food shelves, and welfare. We still weren't making ends meet. Could things get much worse than that? Absolutely!

Chapter 4: My Sacrifices for Family

 I was graduating from the 9th grade and ready to start my summer and then enter the 10th grade in school. One evening we were sitting at the dinner table. My parents told me how badly they were suffering, and that we were in financial ruin, which of course I already knew.

My parents told me that they hated to ask me, but they needed me to quit high school to go to work and help support the family financially. I hesitantly agreed.

Part of me did not mind at all as I saw that my family desperately needed my help and I loved them. The other part of me felt uncomfortable with the idea as I thought about other aspects. What about me? What about what I needed? Why is this happening to us? Did my parents really ask me to give up my education and my future? I was shocked and didn't see that coming.

Shortly thereafter, I ended up quitting high school to go to work and financially support my parents.

Insight #8: I was a loyal loving son who was very family oriented. I couldn't walk away and let my family sink.

I obtained my first job when I was 15 years old. That job was as a dishwasher in a restaurant. I made very little money but worked 60-80 hours per week. Then, in an effort to make more money, I quit my job to go to work for a supermarket.

My job at the supermarket was to stock shelves, work in the freezer, and unload the trucks. I delivered groceries to customers using a bicycle that the supermarket owned. I still did not make enough money to support the family.

Insight #9: Despite my sacrifices and best efforts, my family and I continued to sink.

While my mother was visiting her mother in North Carolina, she asked her mother for help, in getting us out of a terrible situation. My mother's parents agreed even though they did not like my father. I am sure they agreed because they loved their daughter and grandchildren.

My parents decided the only thing they could do is to try and start a new life by moving to North Carolina. We would have to leave what family we had in Massachusetts.

While my mother was in North Carolina visiting her mother, my father had come home from work one day, sat in his recliner, and said that he did not feel well, and was going to go to sleep and rest for a while. I said "OK", and went into my room to play guitar.

My father called me out of my room to tell me that he was having trouble breathing, and that I better call an ambulance. So I called 911. I was 15 years old at the time and had to deal with a medical emergency all by myself. I was scared. It felt like an eternity waiting at the fence for the ambulance so I could direct them into the apartment. My father's eyes rolled in the back of his head and he lost consciousness.

The ambulance arrived, and much to my surprise, my brother, who was a paramedic showed up as one of the paramedics. He wasn't supposed to answer a medical emergency call for his own family but he insisted and was allowed to. I felt comforted by my brother being there. It was a miracle my brother was even there. The paramedics began working on my father.

My father was transported by ambulance and I rode along in the ambulance. I asked my brother "Do you think dad will be alright?" He replied, "We are doing everything we can; we have high hopes of him being ok."

 I remember seeing the medical staff wheel my father down that long sterile hospital hallway down to the emergency room. I remember thinking, why am I

left standing here all alone dealing with a medical emergency at 15 years old? Is my father going to die? What would I do then?

Insight #10: This was a moment that taught me to worry about what might happen instead of waiting until things happen and deal with reality.

Back in the emergency room, my father was diagnosed with emphysema and Chronic Obstructive Pulmonary Disease (C.O.P.D.) from years of smoking. As it was described to me, they had a spike type thing attached to the end of a tube. My father had to push toward them and they pushed towards my father's chest to insert the tube in his chest to re-inflate his lung. Then they admitted him to the hospital, and I visited my father for a while.

My father was admitted to the hospital and then gave me all the money he had in his wallet. He asked me to go food shopping for the family, which I had not done before. My father called my mother to let her know that he was in the hospital and she asked "Should I come home?" Dad replied, "Do whatever you want." She stayed another week, until her vacation was over. I asked my father, "Why didn't you tell her that you wanted her to come home?" He stated that he did not want to ruin her vacation, and she doesn't get to see her family often.

A week later, my father finally came home from the hospital, and all he saw was mostly junk food. He questioned me and was angry with me. I was only 15 years old but I apologized for not doing a good job.

Insight #11: I can't seem to be good enough or do well enough.

A week later, my mother came back from North Carolina. I thought, how could she not come home and leave me to handle everything by myself? After mom's return and after she had talked to her mom, we decided to have a yard sale, we sold all of our furniture including the living room set. It still ended up that we still didn't have enough money to move, so we continued living in the apartment we rented, without most of our furniture.

Chapter 5: My World Is Continuing to Crumble

We still could not survive, and now sold most of our furniture. We still could not afford our apartment, even with all my sacrifices. It was just not good enough. So we got evicted and ended up living with one of the neighbors.

The neighbor was a single mom with a daughter around my age. While I was sleeping on their couch, the daughter kissed me on the lips and my father saw that happen. My father must have gotten nervous about that and maybe scared of losing what little financial support they had in what I was providing, so my father started planning for us to leave. I didn't want to leave. I needed something that felt good to me for a change. Anything that felt good was a welcome change as I knew turmoil and hardship all too well.

So, my parents found a very cheap four door car that I purchased, and a small little Scotty Trailer that hooks up to the back of my car. We installed a trailer hitch on the car. We were now officially homeless. We surpassed being homeless and living with another family. This is when you know who your real friends and family are. We were now out on the street homeless. Could things possibly get any worse? That is a question I should not have asked.

Our very tiny trailer was now a house to us. The trailer had no running water, no electricity, and no heat. We would have to park it out on the street and walk up the street to the bakery in the morning just to wash ourselves. We had no way to take showers. We usually only had enough for a cup of coffee for each of us. Once in a while we had enough for a doughnut. The owner of the bakery knew we were homeless and sometimes helped us by donating a cup of coffee and a doughnut.

People didn't like it that we parked our trailer on their street or in front of their house. In the middle of the night, they would throw lit firecrackers on our trailer from their balcony to frighten us. We would move to another street, and either the same thing would happen or the police would come and tell us we had to move the trailer. We would explain to the police that we had no place to go but that we would move the trailer. We also told the police that we are not hurting anyone.

We decided to find an open lot to park our trailer in. We ended up finding an open lot that no one was parking in and decided to park the trailer there. My mother had gone out to bingo for the night, not that we could afford that, however, that was her only outlet.

She would argue with my father until he gave her twenty dollars so she could go to play Bingo. While she was out that night, it was after dark and there was no lighting in the parking lot. We heard a car speeding outside and screeching and then all of a sudden we heard a loud bang and felt the trailer tipping. It was like God held it up from tipping on its side because it was certainly tipping to the point where it should have fallen on the ground. We realized someone tried to kill us and we were afraid for a very long time after that traumatic event.

In an effort to make a little more money, my father called in a favor and got me a new job working at the factory where my father used to work. I had no choice in the matter and was forced to take this job. My father told me "Whatever you do, don't tell them we are homeless."

At the factory, we made flexible cable for lighting and lightbulbs for chicken coops. I went to work every day. I never called in sick and was never late for work. I dreaded going to work much of the time. I worked there for about six months.

M.T. Stein was married, an alcoholic, bisexual and was having an affair at work. The whole factory suspected and knew about this.

M.T. Stein would go around the factory and tell all the guys that they were doing a great job and would tap them on the ass as he walked away. I left work to go back to where our tiny trailer was parked. I told my father that M.T. Stein tapped me on the ass. My father told me, "Just take it, we need the money".

That made me feel crappy, uncared for and unprotected. My dad didn't even get angry about it. I continually worked as hard as I could to keep this job. I worked as much overtime as I could when it was available.

Insight #12: It felt like my father didn't care about me. I felt like I was just a meal ticket at this point. I was a way to survive. But I knew that both my parents were stuck. I also understood the importance of keeping my job and being consistent at work for the sake of survival.

Chapter 6: Hardship, Help and Humiliation

One day I went to work and upon arriving at work, I was asked to come into the manager's office. I asked, "Is something wrong?" The factory foreman and manager replied, "Yes, we are getting complaints that you have body odor."

I had to explain that I couldn't help it. They replied, "What do you mean you can't help it? Just take a shower." I explained that we were homeless. They didn't believe me. They asked me where the trailer was located. I told them where it was located even though my father told me not to say anything. I was fearful that I would have been fired, if I didn't tell them what they wanted to know.

Because they didn't believe my story, they sent the union steward from the factory to where I said the trailer was located. The union steward went to the trailer, knocked on the door and my parents answered the trailer door. I wasn't privy to the conversation they had but my father wasn't very happy with me for telling them. Later my father told me that it was alright. What choice did he really have at that point? What choice did I really have? It was already done.

While I was working, the company decided to pass around a collection plate, and collected money for us right in front of me. I felt embarrassed to be present while they did that. As they passed the collection plate around, I could see people pointing and talking as they gave money to the cause. My family and I were the cause.

I felt completely humiliated and wanted to just crawl under a rock and die. I wondered if my parents really understood my sacrifice. Did they really understand the lifelong affects that all this would have on me? Did it really matter as long as we had survival? Did they even care? These were things that I felt and thought. I was crushed and embarrassed.

Regardless, I kept going to work every day. The company raised $800 and gave that to us to help some with our survival. The next day,

I was brought into the office and was told that the company wanted to put us up in a hotel and provide us with meals until we could all decide next steps. I of course agreed, as we had no choices. We were thinking that this was quite kind of the company to do that for us and we were thankful for this.

As time went on, we felt like a burden and wondered what the company thought of us. We wondered what the next steps would be as we knew the company couldn't possibly keep this up financially. Again, I went to work and the manager called me into the office. I had been called into the office so often that I dreaded going to work. This caused me such great anxiety, stress and discomfort that I did not feel well most of the time.

I found myself in a meeting with my manager and Human Resources. I thought I was about to be fired. My manager in front of Human Resources stated that the company can't afford to pay for our meals and hotel long term. My response was communicating that we realized that and expressed thankfulness for the help that we have received from the company. I imagine they already felt stuck with us. I was waiting for the bomb to drop and was expecting to be fired.

My manager asked me "Is there any place that you and your family would like to relocate to?" I replied. "Yes, we could either move to North Carolina where my mother's parents live or Minnesota where one of my brothers live." The manager asked me to go to the hotel and decide where you would like to move to and we would talk tomorrow.

After work, I went to the hotel and discussed this with my parents, and we decided to move to North Carolina. However, we decided to first go to Minnesota along the way. We decided to move in with my brother who lived in Minnesota until we could decide next steps.

The next day, I went to work and an hour into my shift, the manager called me into the office. Once again, the manager and Human Resources was at the meeting. The manager asked, "Did you decide about relocation?" I replied, "Yes, Minnesota would be a place we would like to relocate to." My manager told me that they would like to assist us in relocating.

They told me that they were willing to give us a $5,000 check to relocate and that they are willing to use one of their semi-trucks and transport all of our belongings to Minnesota. My manager told me "In return, we would like you to sign a paper stating that if you ever return to Massachusetts, that you will never ask us for a job again." I felt incredibly hurt by this, but we had no choices. I reluctantly signed the paper, and went back to the hotel and cried for a few hours. Life felt so overwhelming many times and this was no exception.

Insight #13: The employer is the enemy and they will hurt you, given a chance. I needed to learn how to trust again and unlearn this insight/lesson.

Chapter 7: Our Departure

We bought bus tickets to relocate to Minnesota as soon as possible. The day arrived that we were to leave, and we were standing waiting for the bus to arrive, we said our goodbyes to all the family that we had in Massachusetts.

We had to say goodbye to my brother, his wife and all the grandchildren. My nephew and I were close which was especially difficult to see him cry so hard. He didn't want to say goodbye and neither did I. We all cried together. We were still crying as the bus departed. I still remember looking out the window with tears rolling down my cheeks as the bus left.

Several days on the bus, we finally arrived in Minnesota and our plan was to move in with my brother until we decide to move on and relocate to North Carolina. We did move in with my brother.

Emotionally we were just not alright. We thought it was hard being homeless. It was even harder saying goodbye and leaving everything we had ever known. We found ourselves in a strange city. To us it was as strange as being in a foreign land. Everything seemed so big compared to where we came from. There was even a bit of culture shock. Food was different, and life was different. I was an East Coast guy who thought everyone in Minnesota spoke perfectly like school teachers. Compared to me, they did. We never did make it to North Carolina.

Chapter 8: Adjusting to A New Life

It was time to start adjusting to a new life. I wondered what we were going to do until we leave Minnesota. How would an uneducated young man with no real skills make money? My brother's house was just enough for his family, but he didn't seem to mind housing us.

So what did it mean to start adjusting to a new life? It meant how to learn to adjust in a new city. We had to learn the bus system, and learn how to get around and navigate a new place. We had to learn what resources were available to us in starting a new life. We had to learn where places were and what there was to do. We had to figure out where we might want to live temporarily until we were ready to move on to North Carolina because we were deciding to stay for a little while longer. We had to learn what jobs were available in a new city and where exactly the locations were.

There were just so many things to figure out and so many things to adjust to. It was eye opening. I think about how I can't imagine what it must be like for people that come to the United States that do not speak English, and have to settle in and adjust. It was quite difficult for us just moving to a new state, with little to no skills, and starting a new life.

Chapter 9: Finally, We Catch a Break

We started looking around for a place to live with a short-term lease so that we could move out of my brother's house before leaving for North Carolina. After looking around for a while, we met this older man that had an apartment for rent. He was willing to offer a six-month lease, although he preferred a year. We rented an apartment from him.

He was a very nice man with a difficult life. He was in his 80's when we met him. He had difficulty getting around and doing the things he used to, so we helped him with certain tasks. My family became friends with him and his wife. His wife was wheelchair bound and loved to drink adult beverages. They would banter back and forth and seemed to have some fun with that.

One day I was talking to him about how I took care of my parents physically and financially and needed to find a job so we don't become homeless again. He said, "Since you're already doing the work, why don't you become a nursing assistant?" So I looked into it and couldn't afford to take the classes to get the certification.

Not long after that, the landlord and I had another conversation. He asked me, "Did you look into taking Nursing Assistant classes and the certification test?" I replied, "I have, but it is not going to work out." He asked me, "Why Not?" I told him, that I don't have the kind of money that they charge for that. He asked how much that they charge. I told him it was $1,500. He told me that he would let me borrow the money. I told him that I didn't know how long it would take me to pay him back. He told me that it would all work out.

So I borrowed the money and became a Nursing Assistant. Over time, I paid him back every penny. I worked 80 hours a week on this job to provide for my parents, to build a new life, and to pay the landlord back. He was such a nice man.

Insight #14: God can provide in unexpected ways.

Chapter 10: Working in
The Nursing Home

I ended up getting a job in a nursing home and worked eighty hours per week most weeks. I figured, if I had to go home and take care of my ill parents, I might as well work as much as I can, caring for other people and get paid for it. I enjoyed helping others and making good money. After all, I had been far down in the pits and I did not want to return there.

I used to get a charge out of the older people and how they reacted and responded. Between working in normal nursing units and working on the Alzheimer unit, it was quite interesting. I looked at this job as a good way to make money. It was also a way to give back to the older generation of people that were in need.

I remember one lady who was tiny, she reminded me of the granny on the Bugs Bunny, Road Runner show. She was sitting in the hall in a big bright orange chair. As people would pass by her, she would quietly mumble swear words that were directed at the person walking past her. We all knew she couldn't help it. We wrote it off and chuckled.

One gentlemen, in particular, used to love to give people a hard time (out of fun) and get a hard time from others. He liked to tease people. I don't really know if he just liked to tease and be teased or if he was trying to get attention when and where he could. Maybe it was a bit of both.

One day I walked by his room and I could hear him giving this black female nursing assistant a difficult time. He would say to her "Get out of here you" and then he used an awful racial slur. She replied in a stern and angry tone, "What did you say to me?" He replied, "Nothing ma'am". So I came into the room and took over the morning tasks and went through our normal banter.

I am remembering asking this guy, "How are you today?" He would reply, "Can't walk, ain't got no teeth". I replied, "You know I like you a lot and think your fun, right?" The man replied, "Yeah".

I proceeded to ask him, "What did you do for a living when you worked?" He said, "I built houses for a living." I said "You did not. Maybe with match sticks." His reply was "I worked hard for a living, damn it". We would continue bantering back and forth and I would guess it was the most fun and interesting part of his day. I still miss him, even to this day. I really liked this man. He was fun, energetic and spicy.

His wife would come into the nursing home, and was abusive to him. I would catch her hitting him. I would come in and tell her visiting time is over and she needs to leave. That was my way of protecting him.

He would cry after she left. I would give him a hug and tell him that I loved him. Everyone needs someone to watch over them and care for them. That is the very reason I had become a nursing assistant. It sure is amazing how certain people can make such an impression on you.

Another lady, who wore oxygen and was pretty much bed-ridden, would take off her oxygen and scream at the top of her lungs, "I can't breathe", as she continued gasping for breath. I saw that as a cry for attention.

There are so many more stories to share, but to share my journey, From Homelessness to Rubbing Elbows with Executives, I wanted to share a few of these stories with you.

Insight #15: You can have fun at work, enjoy your job and make a difference.

Chapter 11: Dating

I remember feeling lonely and not having companionship with the opposite sex. Growing up, I never had a chance to hang out with the guys. I never had a chance to date much. I had two girlfriends in my life. One was back in Massachusetts before we became homeless and the other was in Minnesota.

What was my relationship like with the girlfriend from Massachusetts? I met her in high school, though my high school career ended up being short-lived given the fact that I had to quit high school to support my parents, only to became homeless. She was my very first girlfriend experience.

We would go over one another's house to spend time with each other. My parents seemed to feel threatened by the fact that I was dating. My girlfriend showed me lots of attention that I enjoyed. It felt exciting, fun and something very new for the first time. I was always giving of myself, and for the first time, I mattered to someone and it wasn't based on what I could do for them.

However, there was a negative part of this experience. My girlfriends mother, would call her names like slut, pig and bitch and would embarrass her in front of me. That was so hurtful to her. I felt bad for her and consoled her.

She drank alcohol and smoked pot with her mother. My father used to be an Auxiliary Police Officer and I asked him what he thought of what was happening. He told me that if the police ever raided that house, that I would get arrested if I was there.

He told me I needed to break up with my girlfriend. I listened to my father and broke up with my girlfriend. Although, I must admit, I wondered if he had ulterior motives for suggesting what he did. I regrettably broke up that relationship. I was sad and missed her.

From time to time, I would walk by her house, in hopes of seeing her but I never did see her. A year later, I met up with her brother, and he said that she was very broken hearted when I broke up with her.

Her brother told me that her mother told her that she is such a screw up, that she couldn't hold onto a nice guy. That is when I found out that she had attempted suicide shortly after. I felt sad and broken hearted that I caused some of that. My father had no idea how much damage his advice had caused.

I found out that she was now living with and being cared for by her grandmother and cousins. So I asked to get together with her and talk. I decided I would pay for the date, and she asked if her cousins could come along. I hesitantly agreed and paid for everyone. I found out that she had become a Jehovah's Witness. I was not knowledgeable about spiritual matters nor did my parents teach me about spiritual matters. You can't teach what you don't know.

My ex-girlfriend and her cousins gave me a book to read. I started reading the book, and my spirit felt so uncomfortable with the beliefs stated in that book. Not being able to give blood if someone needed a blood transfusion. This was in conflict with what was in my heart and soul. I went back to her grandmother's house, placed the book at the foot of the door, and simply walked away. That was not an easy thing to do. Eventually, I had become homeless and needed to relocate to Minnesota.

How did I meet my girlfriend in Minnesota? Well, she worked at the same nursing home that I did. One day, I went into the utility room, and there were this person's feet, wiggling with the laundry shoot shut on them. We were on the third floor. So, I grabbed one leg with one hand, and opened the laundry shoot with the other hand, and pulled her out of the laundry shoot. That is how we met. For only the second time in my life, I felt that sparkle and feeling of excitement. But this time, something felt different for me. It was accompanied by much joy and happiness.

Every time we would go to our homes, I couldn't wait to be with her again. It was always hard to say goodbye. This lasted for about a year and a half. I think when this lasts for that long, you know you love this person and if they experience the same, maybe that is a sign that you belong together.

My girlfriend asked me to come by the church and listen to her sing in the choir. I didn't have much experience with God at this point. The choir director sat by me, and asked me my name, he wrote it down. Then he asked my address and telephone number and he wrote that down. He said, "Congratulations, you just joined choir." I started going to choir and church weekly. My father told me I was too much into this Jesus thing and that I was becoming a Jesus freak. I felt proud of myself for embracing Jesus.

Chapter 12: Meet the Parents

After dating for a while, it was now time for each of us to meet the parents. My girlfriend's parents were educated people who worked in ministry and education and were in good health. My parents did not have a formal education but were certainly educated in life. They were retired out of necessity and not in good health.

After meeting my girlfriend's family, their family dynamics were very different from what I was used to. They seemed like nice people, spiritual people, quite successful financially, owned their own home, had vehicles, went on vacations and helped their children succeed with education. Again, very different than what I had experienced in my life. I felt unequal to them. They had a relationship with God, and I didn't even know what that was all about. The families did not even seem compatible.

After much discussion with my girlfriend about these differences, we discussed that the two families may not be compatible, but we are. We also discussed the financial differences. I was concerned that I wouldn't be able to provide at the level she was probably accustomed to. Her reply was, "We will figure everything out." She was fine with that. I believed her and was right to believe her. We continued dating and enjoying one another.

When my girlfriend met my family, my parents were unhappy. When it became known that the relationship was getting serious, my mother said to me, "Are you trying to kill your father?" My reply was, "No, I am trying to be happy and create my own family with the person I am meant to be with."

After dating for some time, it was time for the parents to meet one another. We were right, they did not seem very compatible. It seemed to me that they were not comfortable with one another but they were cordial. We had gotten quite serious and announced to our parents that this relationship was very serious and we are talking about marriage.

My mother said to me, "If you marry into that family, you will be sorry." Maybe they were concerned about survival. After all, this was not the first time, these kinds of attitudes and feelings surfaced.

Chapter 13: Starting a Family

As I had planned, I had asked my girlfriends father out of respect for his blessing before asking for his daughters hand in marriage. He had given his blessing after having a discussion with me. I stopped into a jewelry store, and picked out an engagement ring so that I could propose to my girlfriend.

We attended Park Avenue United Methodist Church and were getting ready to sing in the Soul Liberation Choir, and as we were standing with the choir on the platform, I proposed to my girlfriend with the rest of the choir standing around us. That was an awesome moment. Now the wedding planning began and we were fully engaged to be married.

Excitement and fun was in the air, and we were excited to be together no matter what problems we might face in the future. We got married and started our family. After working in the nursing home for a while, I started working in retail. I didn't make much money but it was a job and I always had a job.

Chapter 14: Continued Education

My girlfriend's father was an associate/youth pastor of the church, and in back of the church was a computer center. My father-in-law encouraged me to go to the computer center and get help studying for my G.E.D. to obtain my high school education.

I started attending the Park Avenue Computer Center and studied diligently for my G.E.D. I studied for several months and the director of the computer center told me that I was now ready to take the test. I remember before taking the test, my wife would test me on the state capitals to make sure I remembered them all.

I called and scheduled a date to take the test at Minneapolis Community College and then nervously showed up that day to take the test. I took the test, and had to wait for my results in the mail.

Finally, the results showed up in the mail. I opened the letter, and it provided all the test scores. I had achieved my G.E.D. Frankly, I did better in the subjects than I had done in school overall. Probably, because I really wanted my high school education since I had no choice earlier in my life but to give up my education for the sake of my family.

Chapter 15: Discovering My Interests and What I Am Good At

Through studying for my G.E.D. at the Park Avenue Computer Center, I found my interest and love for technology. I took classes such as Introduction to Computers, DOS, Lotus, Microsoft Office etc.

I bought local newspapers, opened the classified ads, and typed the entire classified ads to increase my typing speed and accuracy. After gaining several certificates, I tried to get a job in the computer field, but was unsuccessful due to not having experience in the computer field.

I was determined to figure out a way to reach my goals.

I kept working on computer and technology skills while working in retail. My passion for technology increased and I continued learning as much as I could about business and technology as I continued on my path to achieve my dreams.

Chapter 16: Discovering Personal Values

I believe wholeheartedly in discovering and understanding our own personal values. As I thought about my values, I understood them to be:

- Accepting Yourself and Situations
- Achieving
- Appreciation
- Asking for Help
- Being Compassionate
- Being Truthful
- Belonging
- Connecting
- Creating
- Daring to Dream
- Embracing the Moment
- Feeling Different
- Feeling Pleasure
- Feeling Secure
- Forgiving

- Imagining
- Letting It Be
- Loving and Being Loved
- Moving – Getting Things Done
- Seeing Possibilities
- Seeking Freedom
- Seeking Knowledge
- Seeking Wisdom
- Staying with Uncertainty
- Struggling
- Trusting
- Understanding
- Words of Encouragement

Again, this is not an exhaustive list, but a good list of determining and understanding my values. We understand our values by what is important to us and they are also based on our story. Everyone has a story and everyone has values. We just need to connect with them and identify what they are.

I would encourage you to work on determining what your values are. What are some values that are important to you? They are part of your foundational belief system. They make you who you are, both good and otherwise. But remember, that they can change over time.

Things you need to unlearn or reshape are not really your values. They are life experiences that have caused you to believe something about yourself that may not be true. So be careful about that piece of determining your values.

Chapter 17: Success and What It Requires

Success requires a lot from a person. I am a self-made man in terms of my success. This means that I invested lots of blood, sweat and tears into my success and my achievements.

Success requires a person to work hard, be diligent, and requires sacrifices. I have sacrificed time, that has required energy, effort, brain power and physical effort. One must be willing to do whatever it takes to succeed, within reason of course. You must stay true to your values if you want to live a life based on your values. This definitely includes your career.

What are you willing to do in order to achieve your dreams and level of success that you desire? Are you willing to get the information and education you need for success? Are you willing to take the steps necessary to make it happen? Are you willing to take the bull by the horns and achieve your dreams?

Chapter 18: Building A New Skill Set

By now you realize that I have worked very hard in my life to get the information and education I needed to succeed in my desired area. Some of the education I have achieved was formal education, and some of the education, I did at my own pace on my own. I made it happen.

One of the ways I made it happen was after I received my certificates from the Park Avenue Computer Center, I had to face facts and realize that I could not get a job in the computer field due to lack of experience. I grabbed the bull by the horns and I went to the local computer store, and bought up their junk pile of computers. We didn't have much money but it was time to see it, believe it, sacrifice and achieve.

I bought a book on how to repair computers and studied it repeatedly. I repaired the computers, installed software, bought some inexpensive printers and sold computer packages. These computer packages consisted of a computer loaded with software, and a color printer.

I placed an ad in the paper, and started selling computers. I was now in the computer field making my own experience happen. This is what I mean by grabbing the bull by the horns and making things happen. As I enhanced this skill set, I also worked on other skills. I learned database design, and how to setup computer networks. As technology evolved, I consistently learned new areas of technology. It really did not feel like work as I loved technology.

The main point here is to find what you are passionate about. Find what you love to do and then go out and make it happen.

Chapter 19: Resume and Interviewing Skills

If I wanted to break into the computer industry as a full time career, I also had to work on creating a resume, and cover letter. I did research, read books and learned how to create a resume. I also received assistance at the Park Avenue Computer Center.

Do whatever you need to, in order to make things happen. Do not be afraid to ask for help when needed to achieve your dreams.

I practiced interviewing skills by role playing interviews with friends and family. I did what I needed to so that I could get good at understanding how to interview. I wanted to become skilled at landing the job of my dreams. I also was realistic and knew that it would be a process and would happen over time. Little did I know, how much time it would take. The time it takes can be different for everyone and maybe it also depends on the path one takes.

Chapter 20: Really Selling Yourself

One of the biggest questions I have been asked, is "How do you ace an interview and land the desired job?" My response is, "You don't look at it as a job and an interview. You look at it as a career and opportunity."

When I go on an interview, I look at it as an opportunity to meet some great people, who have a need that I can help them with, long term. They are not just interviewing me to see if I am a good fit for the career and company, but I am interviewing them to see if they are people that I want to work with as well.

I think about certain questions as I am being interviewed and interviewing them. Are they a company that I feel that I can be successful working with? Does the company as a whole value their employees? Can I grow in this company? Will I be satisfied performing the duties of this opportunity for quite some time? Can I make a difference and an impact?

You must know the things you bring to the table and the value you will not only bring to the opportunity but to the company as well. You must put a price tag on your skills and value that you bring overall.

In order to have a successful interview, you must be a people-person and connect with the people that you meet with. People hire who they like. They are assessing if you can perform the duties that they need you to perform. They are also assessing how well you will fit within the company. Be adaptable and sincere in the interview.

Chapter 21: Paying Your Dues

Paying your dues means that I have sacrificed lots of things. All the way from childhood to adulthood. I have sacrificed dating, hanging out with the guys, my education, being a kid, leading a successful and normal life as well as many other aspects.

I have worked at many jobs that I did not like and that did not pay well. I worked at many jobs that had awful hours and offered no benefits just to make ends meet. Paying my dues also meant working at the bottom rung and working my way up the technology ladder one job opportunity at a time.

I had to do lots of internal searching of my wants, needs, passions and always assessing myself and the value that I am bringing to an employer. I always had to work hard at learning new skills and performing new tasks.

Insight #16: There is a price to pay for success, but it is worth the investment.

Chapter 22: Breaking into an Industry

After starting my own business and working for a while fixing and selling computers, I decided to put that experience on my resume and see if I could start a career in the technology industry.

I received my first break and was hired as a technical support representative helping people resolve their hardware and software technical issues. Then I continued getting opportunities in the areas of support, database design, computer networking, and a variety of opportunities that continually increased my skills.

I have had opportunities to do some great tasks throughout my career. I had an opportunity where I was promoted from technical support representative to Technology Manager. In this opportunity, I worked for a computer manufacturer working with the production team to track and fix technology issues manufacturing the computers.

Part of my job was to hire, mentor and train staff to resolve computer issues for consumers purchasing computers. I also would work with the Valu-Vision Home Shopping Network Call Center. I would run around the call center and answer technical questions prior to consumers purchasing their computer. I would train the call center on how to do the computer upgrade shows.

I then designed a web based Intranet design solution for the company that I worked for, and created a web-based technical support knowledge base for the technical support department and production department.

Chapter 23: One Thing Leads to Another

In 2003, one thing leads to another and I fell into the area of Technology Consulting. I landed a consulting position with 3M and fell into Microsoft SharePoint design. 3M sent me to a SharePoint site owners class so that I could learn SharePoint inside and out. I found that I really enjoyed Microsoft SharePoint and wanted to continue learning more about that technology.

So I start designing and customizing more solutions using Microsoft SharePoint. I started meeting with teams throughout the organization in the United States region, gathering requirements, and implementing solutions. Before I knew it, I had developed a new skill set. I was now performing as a Business Analyst, SharePoint Developer and Technical Writer in delivering project solutions accompanied by documentation. Although, I spent many hours on my own, evenings and weekends, honing my skills.

Chapter 24: Rubbing Elbows with Executives

Throughout the years, I continued working in SharePoint since 2003. I worked as a consultant through all the different versions of SharePoint. I worked with SharePoint 2003, 2007, Business Productivity Office System (BPOS), 2010, 2013 and Office 365.

At this point, I had gained a few more skill sets such as Project Management, and Trainer. Now, I could say that I deliver a complete package of services for any company that brings me on board as a consultant or an employee. When you hire me, you are getting a SharePoint Developer, Business Analyst, Technical Writer, Project Manager and Trainer. This is worth real money and I worked hard over many years and paid my dues to get to this point.

I have worked side by side with executives of small companies, large corporations, and government organizations. I found myself working with teams, managers, directors, Vice Presidents and Chief Executive Officers.

I had now come a long way from being homeless in Massachusetts. I had increased my income significantly and reached a higher tax bracket. I realized, that with these skill sets, I would never be homeless again.

I did not only achieve career success, but I had an important story to tell. I had something to share that could help and inspire others in their life. I knew it was time to share my story and let others know, if I can do it, they can too.

Then my dreams expanded which usually happens as we get older in our lives. We end up maturing, growing and changing. My dreams expanded to become an author, and life coach. I am now beginning to realize those dreams and bring them to life. Life is good and it can be good for you too.

Chapter 25: Defining/ Refining Goals

Defining and refining your goals are not always easy. The first thing that you want to do is make sure that all your goals are yours. Sometimes it is hard because you think you want something, however, the truth is you're doing it for someone else.

Or maybe it's something that you think you should want to do or would be good for you, even if it's not what you want, or the fact that you're just not that interested in it.

However well-meaning you or others might be, you will not be committed to goals that don't inspire or energize you. This is not about doing what you think you should do. This is about exploring what inspires and energizes you. This is about exploring your future. These are your own goals for yourself.

Remember to live in the present. Think about your goals in the present tense. Create them and think about them as if they are happening here and now, not in the future. Define, redefine and think about your goals in the framework of actively achieving them now.

It might seem strange at first, but you need to speak it into existence. Words are powerful.

This is important because it sends a strong signal with clarity to your mind that this is your reality.

Keep your thoughts and messages positive. Frame your statements in the positive not the negative. Make sure you say what you want. Don't say what you don't want. Once again, this sends a message with clarity to your brain. It is more effective to state the intended result rather than interpreting what something you don't want may look like.

Remember that It's difficult to think about and measure something that is negative or something that doesn't exist. Something that is positive and can be imagined and is desired is more measurable and more likely to lead you to activities and actions that focus on your preferred outcome.

Start out with purpose. Bring clarity to the reasons why you are doing what you are doing. This is crucial to creating goals that are inspiring to you. The purpose behind your goals is what will be your motivation and serve you well.

Make sure that whatever lies behind you wanting to achieve your goals are so important to you that it will inspire, energize and sustain your commitment to accomplishing them.

Dream big, because the bigger your 'why' the easier it will be to stay committed to achieving your goals and dreams.

You will work best and be most happy when you have a sense of purpose and direction.

It is critical to write out your goals. In writing down your goals, you define and declare them. What you are doing here is clearly stating your new intention and in doing so you start to shift your focus and energy onto the actions and opportunities that will coincide with getting you on track towards your vision and mission in life.

Chapter 26: Beginning to Discover and Live Out Your Dreams

Remember that everything begins in your heart and in your mind. You need to dare to dream just like we talked about in the values section of this book. You need to believe that it is possible.

Ask yourself, "What if?" Think big. Don't be discouraged by negative thinking. Dream! Dream of all the possibilities for yourself, your family and others.

If you had a dream that has not come to fruition or you let grow cold, re-ignite the dream!

You need to believe in yourself and your dreams. Your dream needs to be big. It needs to be something that is seemingly beyond your capabilities. But it also must be believable. You must be able to say that if certain things take place, if others help, if you work hard enough, though it is a big dream, it can still be done.

See your dreams. The great achievers have a habit. They "see" things. They picture themselves walking around in their dream as if they had already achieved their dreams.

Tell your dreams. One reason many dreams never go anywhere is because the dreamer keeps it all to them self. It is a quiet dream that only lives inside of their mind.

The one who wants to achieve their dream must tell that dream to many people. As we say it, we begin to believe it. If we are talking about it then it must be possible. It holds us accountable. When we have told others, it leads us to actually doing it so we don't look foolish.

Plan it. Every dream must take the form of a plan. Your dream won't just happen. You need to sit down, on a regular basis, and plan out your strategy for achieving the dream. Think through all of the details. Break the whole plan down into small parts. Then set a time frame for accomplishing each task.

Be willing and ready to work really hard to achieve your dreams. Unfortunately, the most successful people are usually the hardest workers. While the rest of the world is relaxing or being entertained, achievers are working on their goals and achieving their dream.

Remember that your short-term tasks, multiplied by time, equal your long-term accomplishments. If you work on it each day, eventually you will achieve your dream.

Enjoy it. When you have reached your goal and you are living your life based on your values and living your dreams, be sure to enjoy it. Be sure to enjoy how you got there. Enjoy the journey. Give yourself some rewards along the way. Help others enjoy it. Be gracious and generous. Use your dream to better others. And dream a little bigger this time!

Printed in the United States
By Bookmasters